D1616972

OTHER HOUSES

OTHER HOUSES

KATE CAYLEY

Brick Books

Library and Archives Canada Cataloguing in Publication

Cayley, Kate, author
Other houses / Kate Cayley.

Poems.
Issued in print and electronic formats.
ISBN 978-1-77131-454-1 (softcover).—ISBN 978-1-77131-456-5 (PDF).—
ISBN 978-1-77131-455-8 (EPUB)

I. Title.

PS8605.A945O84 2017   C811'.6   C2016-907497-8
                                        C2016-907498-6

We acknowledge the Canada Council for the Arts, the Government of Canada
through the Canada Book Fund, and the Ontario Arts Council for their support of
our publishing program.

The author photo was taken by Carmen Farrell.
The book is set in Scala.
The cover image is by Peeter Viisimaa.
Design and layout by Marijke Friesen.
Printed and bound by Sunville Printco Inc.

Brick Books
431 Boler Road, Box 20081
London, Ontario
N6K 4G6

www.brickbooks.ca

For Lea

Contents

Writers' Bedrooms

Other Houses

The Library of the Missing

Writers' Bedrooms

The Pied Piper Enchants the Rats

Mutton, crumbs, rotted heart of the house
Call you home

Grey smear of lard, stink-end of cheese
Call you home

The stuffing you rip from pillows, nest of sheets and goose down
Call you home

I, peacock-bright, needle-sharp, red-heeled, bead-eyed
Call you home

The churning whorls of the water,
Drops of water on your whiskers, rising water
Call you home.

Here is the water: swimming with your pretty pink paws
You find the place you sought.

The stream is for you, I am for you, my pipe is for you, I lay
Myself in service to you, there is no love like mine,

Here is the splashing and the surge, the lightness
Of the swimmer. You are so tired from the earth,
You sink under. My music carried with you—

Humming in your furry ears, everything I promise
Waiting for you on the riverbed.

A Partial List of People Who Have Claimed to Be Christ
Ann Lee, 1736–1784

I will not sit in your presence, persecutors. Bare-headed
before you I stand examined, men of English church, men of
holy cloth, but I was a seamstress, snipping lives in my fingers.

I could rip a seam like the ocean, which I aim to cross, leading
my women and men, who sweat alike and walk together, for only
by the sameness of men and women shall either be redeemed.

When I shudder, you will say the fit is on me, and mock me,
but I say you are filth, to see filth. I shake with the Word, myself
Mother Ann, female form of Christ. My babies dead, my womb

blasted, God knew I was for other offers. Not for me
the spindle, the bed. Shake your heads, churchmen. I see
you titter as the rabble does. Do not touch me. I will burn

your hands with holiness. Ask me any point of theology
and I will answer you in tongues. Cut mine out, I will speak.
I will inherit. I will turn the world upside down.

"I should have been a pair of ragged claws"

And if, then, you are. Scuttling
and seeking, predatory

pincers, crabwise, all
eyes and appetite, undulations

of water and bone. The light
bursting above,

the sand ridged, your spines
and back fearful of cracking,

your claws pressing prey.
You are terror

and beauty, your indifference
perfect. You eat

and move, and will be
broken and scattered,

rolling along the cool floors
and forests of weedy light,
waving under water.

Hans Christian Andersen Becomes Acquainted with
His Shadow

Waking among the bedsheets, a talkative man
chastened to silence. Prudishly dreaming, pruning
himself away from unspeakable love, refracted into fame:
that queer consolation, a useful alchemy, giving
every shameful thing a different sheen.

Outside the window, tick drop, tick drop, clock
choruses with melting ice, darkness blooms at the bed-foot,
and he has used up all his matches. Nothing but burnt stubs.
He hears it. That humiliating other, chuckling. Some claw

reaching forward. There must be a light
somewhere. Or he would not see it. The cackle
almost worded, but not quite. When it speaks
he knows it will be well-spoken. Otherwise
it would not be his.

The ice, in the harbour below, breaking.

"Housewife" Revised

The house: a pod
waiting on a twig. Patient spider, praying
mantis, female legs rubbing dry, dry
sticks. Cocoon, chrysalis, cockroach

rustling in the cupboard. Embarrassment
of scurrying disorder, that quick
reflex at the sink when a centipede
breaks stride out of the narrow drain.

You pause, sluicing water
down the dark coil after the hundred legs, watch
the agony of drowning, feathering feet older
than your first ancestor, so easily dismissed.

The house knows you
only in passing, impermanent invader,
your children clattering on
dirty stairs, curious shoes crowding the hall.

The house will keep you. It will not remember you.
It's an animal breathing, staring
at you through the bars. A fury checked
for the present.

Lift the latch, duck your head inside. It is
roomier than you thought. The light
is not bad. The animal
might sleep beside you, be you.

Lie down on the straw.

Arthur Conan Doyle and Harry Houdini Share Breakfast

Cunning man, and wise enough to keep up the patter, Doyle
lays plots. Houdini listens, keeping his eyes
somewhere else, pointing his host the wrong way. Look here,
not here, where the trick nests. By the time the eye
swerves back, it's done. What's meant to vanish, has.

The teaspoons are gone. Doyle is determined
not to be hoodwinked, outwitted. He's canny, genial, disposed
to liking the chicanery that lends itself to art. He blinks
and his toast rack has evaporated. Both are too polite
to mention this. Consummate gentlemen

revisioning their ancestry: rueful Irishman, shamed Jew, knowing
they may inherit through ostensible obedience, press hard
on the mold, secretly break it. Doyle rises, coughing lightly,
and flings the net. Houdini dodges, dives under the table
but his feet are already shackled. Doyle smiles,

swilling laughter. Then sees appearing on the tablecloth
among the china roses and the crumbs, sudden
other objects: sealed letter, straitjacket, noose.
Pocket watch, deathwatch beetle, death's head.

He ducks his head down just in time
to see Houdini wriggle free, brandishing cuffs,
whistling through the gap in his teeth. Cards
erupt from the napkin holder, Tarot showing one
or another face. Empress and Hanged Man,

World and Fool. Staring over the muffins, eggs,
bread and butter, they make a truce, saying
nothing. Fear death by water. Fear the end.
Yet neither does, and so they nod,
knowing that each may apprehend the other.

About a Poem I Read Once

A brooch. A mirror. A girl
comes seeking into an empty house.
Walls crumble at her foggy breath.

It has been winter a long time, more than
any orderly season. The house in the middle
of a wood, branches lattice the spare light.

Homeless in her icy house, she unmuffles
in front of the mirror.
A brooch at her throat.

In the mirror, the brooch becomes an eye.
The eye opens. She sees what it is.
I don't recall whether the house

remained empty. Whether another face rose up
behind her, wolf or sorcerer or perilous
mother, only recently dead.

Whether she was blessed with a sign, and went on.
Or stayed. The eye becomes a mouth, and speaks.

Outside, it begins to snow.

A Partial List of People Who Have Claimed to Be Christ
Arnold Potter, 1804–1872

Here we are. The cliff edge, open before me. Do not crowd
about me, or I will lose footing. I will not whisper, you shall hear
me loud. Remember, baptized in Switzerland County I shouted
to heaven and now heaven
begins to shout back. I have marked my forehead,

scored it over and over until the ink failed, and I bled black.
Written there: *I am Potter Christ.* You that are humbled may read.
Others I cast down into hell. My followers are few, but OUR LORD
had only twelve, and one of them traitorous.

My beloved children, the way up is narrow.
I kiss your hearts, you black-robed men, women
who have ceased to comb your hair. I myself have stopped
shaving; it is unseemly. Let your beards droop in the mud.

I bless the lice upon your scalps, the packed clay under your nails.
Here, in your sight, I will ascend. Watch me leap. Only the ignorant
will say I fell. Do not give in to despair if I seem to drop, do not wail
at the brokenness of my body. Do not take up combs

or any work, or busy yourselves with private sorrows. Preach
in my stead, apostles. I will watch from heaven,
laughing and laughing. Stand back. I sprout wings.

David Bowie in Drag, "Boys Keep Swinging" Video, 1979

Reincarnated as his immaculate other, he becomes
his mother's generation.

Keeping up a body is a battle with the world: self
snared and fixed, a serious business. That beige skin

will not admit cold or doubt. Preservation
in wartime, a way of winning when you lose.

I'm not the woman he is, but admire
such emulation. Knowing,

meant. Chip on the shoulder, taking it
on the chin. The woman he is

pours a drink at four, serves dinner
in heels. Wig plucked off, lipstick

raising a red bruise, granny
lolloping over into wolfishness.

We're in on the secret, aren't we?
Even as we're eaten.

Inkwell

If he'd lost his arms, she might have said no.
Or he might not have asked.

Inscribed inkwell, empty. Homecoming gift
for a great-grandfather, 1919. So scarred his son swore
that when his father wore a bathing suit you couldn't see
three inches of unbroken skin. His hands
full of holes. Why give him an inkwell?

In the prison camp, he wrote
and asked her to marry him, captive
dictating to a German nurse,

his arms saved from amputation
by a Jewish doctor, who kept
in touch with him until the thirties, then letters
were returned to sender. My life owed
to that man's anonymous bones.

We make language, but mostly
we make things. Our objects
live longer, are more absolute
than words.

Stuff crushingly immune to death:
dung beetle, Sisyphus.

What's touched
outlasting any hand that touches it.

Still here. Each year
each owner knowing less, as significance sloughs
away, burns off, but the thing stays
and stays, becoming, without us, only itself.

Other Houses

Pied Piper: The Children, Leaving, Sing to Their Parents

Why are you surprised?

We heard
a singing in the wood.

Our eyes are brighter than the rats. We, too,
are built of curiosity and appetite, we vibrate
what we touch, how could we not
follow the man in patches,

leaving you excavated,
your streets
quiet as you wished for.

We've made ourselves now,
following the pipe, the door
that opens in the hill, which you

hung back from, cowards. You were made
to make us, nothing else.

Write our names in the window each night.

Inscribed in churches, and furtively in the kitchen steam
the kettle makes against the glass. Etch us
on the hollow glass of your own hearts.

Don't look for us, though. We don't look for you.

Shadow

> *Everyone carries a shadow, and the less it is embodied in the individual's*
> *conscious life, the blacker and denser it is.* —C. G. Jung

Wear it like a hat. Plunge your hands in deep pockets. Shuffle
sideways, see what streams past you, longer and longer, other dancer.

You can't, like Jung, spend your days building stone castles
and knocking them over, to find a calmness

of making and unmaking. Understand that the stone will not regret
breaking you. You will break. You will, like him, dream

streams of blood, underground river, slow boat poling along,
and the dead face in black water, rising up

to meet you, open mouth, slate-chip eyes staring
at the spectre of your own missed heroics, your failures

of grace. Touch the skin, pale moon, frog's gullet.
The lids will not shut. Wake. Like Jung,

try to remember. There, you almost saw it, whiskering
away behind you, following.

Hoist it. You'll caterwaul at the weight,
but stagger, swing low, and it's almost a dance step.

Burying My Grandmother

I'm told
the rings and stubborn bits of bone
are removed
before the small box is buried.

One piece resists fire, another gives in.
Something in that knuckle, shin, hip splinter
that will not capitulate, the way she kept
his name after the marriage ended. He
barely spoke hers.

We use our hands. Three generations
from that blasted root, pale brown dirt
under our fingernails. Improbable that we
are her, and she's the box.

Bitterness and blondness, gaunt
years where something
hopeful flickered. Tenacious
and refused love. We threw earth over it.

Daedalus and Icarus

He dreamed his son was a bird.

It was a pardonable thought.
Fathers think these things,
mulling possibilities, noting
a body outlined in the fridge light,
the thwack of a door, a sudden
ability for numbers, words.

His son hollow-boned, red-
feathered, fearless. Fledged.
Bright-eyed, already aloft
as though bypassing human
muscularity, the lumbering frame,
the lolling head.

After the fall into the sea
his father was stooped forever,
as though looking in each pavement crack
for that closing hole in the water below him.

If only he'd spoken differently.
If he'd imparted his own
shortcomings. Soldered his son
to earth. Yet it seemed
too much to waste, that winged hope
in hell, ascending.

In Which I Am Sir Gawain Beheading the Green Knight

I heard it first as green night.

Pictured poison
rising from a wet hollow, the crook of the land
fuming in near-evening.

Last light tipped back and vanishing. Green
throughout the waiting valley. Hoofbeats falling on stone

as the green horse is reined in, knight and I strike
together, match and flint.

The sword's a struggle, awkward wedge of metal, nearly
dislocating arm from shoulder. I lack the equipment
to think of the blade as part of me. But
I don't do too badly—

his neck clean as plucked poultry, and I
heave home, cleaving
flesh from bone,
gap widening: mouth grinning
and then a halved sausage and then nothing—

snapped pencil, blood cedar-dark on larch-green skin.

Cool cucumber, he picks up
his own head, solid as a bowling ball. Loose skin
flapping, brave and brazen dream of peril and warning.

And all around him the green night, gathering.

A Partial List of People Who Have Claimed to Be Christ
William W. Davies, 1833–1906

One coin in the cap, let silver strike silver,
grief and debt turn to bread. Walk on, then,
if you must. You will come again. Everything comes

again, and what is, was. See the evidence
of branch and leaf, snow falling and melting,
covering and revealing the land. There is no original shape,
no final death. A coin. Look
how they hang together. I knew they would. What
I see, I have seen, what I know, I have known.

I am, or have been, the Archangel Michael; my son Arthur,
the second Christ. Praise him. When he was birthed
I lifted him to my heart, and felt his beat outstrip me—
he knew himself the Living God. My younger son, David,
was God the Father. I sat by the throne of my children
and led the congregation: holy, holy, holy, holy—

Diphtheria entered those singing mouths.
Both my boys died within a night, chasing each other
down the mortal rope, umbilical cord in reverse
hoisting them to heaven, their throats burst.

That's worth another coin. My followers
are faithless. Walk on, until you turn again
to me. I am the old man of San Francisco,
with nothing but time.

Antoni Gaudí Looks at a Leaf While Designing the
Sagrada Familia

He is not finished. He will
not live to finish. Nothing
that lives is finished.

He sees it in tree branches. They
are all still too short.

The leaf unfurls, pushing
through etched veins. It will fall
shortly.

If only a church could be
a leaf, he thinks, hiding his head
against the dead wood of his desk.

Or the desk grow, again, the tree.

I should make a window like
a leaf, he thinks, like
that leaf. That leaf. Nothing will be
so green or gold again.

His hair is black wire, conducting heat. What
stirring in the maze behind his eyes. I must
prune myself, he thinks, or I will grow

a tree out of my head. The floor
of this room will be littered with cut branches.

Skull: A History

Jabbering kernel, mind's eye,
the hallowed house, making the perilous

passage through the birth canal.
Seat of the world.

Fortress of bone.
Cavern, brain-cradle.

Self-hood. We've been
through a lot together,
though not much

out of the ordinary, white dome
protected, still-secret.

Indifferent to me,
bearing no distinguishing

marks, and would,
tossed on a pile, seem

the same as anyone's.
Like knocking against like,

bare as a table,
clean as a whistle.

A Walk After Dark, 1966

Sick of wilderness, Pan proceeds along the pavement,
appearing to that rare creature, elderly solitary man who lives
with a murmuring heart and a thousand books.

And what was Pan doing, not
as thought, down in the reeds by the river, but
on the city street, lapped in the loping night, walking
beside the man, neither Death nor Christ?

Pan purrs darkness. Pipeless, his hooves alone
beat time against the stone. They walk a little way
together. The man understands: this is the walk
for which he has been saved, each year
teaching patience. Faith of libraries, waiting
for these five minutes, the world's unbroken egg
temporally his. *Do you love me?*
asks the god, and the man cries, *Yes,*
and he turns the corner and is again alone.

Mannequin

You'd need a saw to mark that skin,
stone god calcified to plastic, lips parted
to breath a rarified flashbulb air.

My daughter yearns to the other side
of the glass: *Look, isn't she beautiful?*
She is so tender, my daughter. Fragile.
Recent scar, emergency room stitches.
Such a casual weave of flesh and bone.

No, you are, I say. Meaning beautiful.
She laughs, wrinkling her nose, scornful
already, divining me
sentimental, unreliable. A liar. Lucky
mannequin, who has and needs no mother.

The Dream of Flight, 1830

Afterwards, nobody could think what it was.
Whatever it was, he heard it. Flap flap flap.
He heard it. There was no going back then.

He built them at night, hoarded feathers—stiff goose, soft
slaughtered rooster. Riffling the ducks by the pond, chased
the ravens and crows crying over the barn. He learned to sew,
sister-teased, until he made them.

Midnight. Balanced on the rooftop, stars pulsing down,
lonely boy, scared of witches and the dark. The crash
woke them all, falling over each other down the stairs
and there—the body crazily skewed over the woodpile.

Broken arms, feathers in his mouth, shuddering
white lips whispered: *I flew.*

The wrists heal crooked. The boy outgrows
his shame. Superstitious,
the family laugh themselves sick, hoping
not to be cursed with too much longing.

His mother watches him, akimbo-
wrists under his chin, listening at night
by the window, dreaming the wind
full of feathers, promising
and lying, promising and lying.

A Partial List of People Who Have Claimed to Be Christ
Laszlo Toth, 1938–2012

The patient is still writing letters to the Pope. He complains of not receiving an answer, though he allows that even great men may be afraid of the unexpected. He went to Rome, he says, for revelation, as it was his thirty-third year. What he did there on Pentecost Sunday, he did with his whole heart. When he struck Michelangelo's *Pietà* with the geologist's hammer he'd hid under his coat, it was a step up from carpentry. He struck first at the Virgin's arm, then nose, then eye, because she would not look at him. Her son.

I lie to him, like all doctors. His followers are waiting for him on the other side of the padded door. He turns to face the wall when he sees me. Some days he says nothing. Other days he begs me for a chisel. He wishes to pry himself apart. His blood will rinse his spirit clean, his guts unwind along the carpet, his bones split like winter wood, and the true part of him will show plainly, risen.

Cumaean Sibyl

Nine.

She wrote with her left hand, through wary
Nights, knowing already
The destiny of each.

Six.

Thetis, holding Achilles over the fire, steeled herself
Less, scorching the small log of his infant body, than she,
Watching as each page softened into ashes,
Curled in her unyielding hands: word's end.

Three.

When she sold them they were still worth
The same as before—volumes
Swollen with the ghosts of those burned books.
She accepted the king's gold, and, counting it, put aside
What was necessary. A coin for the boatman.

The Library of the Missing

The Library of the Missing

A History of the Library

The Library of the Missing was founded in 1884 by Ezekiel Mason, and endowed in perpetuity through his bequest. As he wrote in a private letter, "I believe that the unsteady boundary between life and death is nowhere evidenced so fully as in the contemplation of the traces of the missing, and thus, through such contemplation, the moral character of our age will be greatly strengthened."

Mason himself went missing in 1897, while travelling on a private train bound for New York, though sightings of him were reported in Europe and South America until 1914, when interest in his fate waned following the outbreak of the First World War.

Mason's disappearance is of course a metaphor for a general sense of loss, or absence, or threat, or unexplainable dread, or sadness. These are the subjects, often, of poetry. It is a somewhat profligate, or at least over-elastic, metaphor.

In a disappearance, there is no body. But how can that be? There is always a body.

Mason's body was plump and benevolent. He often wore fur. He had a long beard. After his disappearance, his daughter Beatrice took over the administration of the library, until her death in 1951, at which point it became a public institution.

The Library expands every year, as it must.

The building is under continual renovation. Despite this constant upheaval, it is also mapped. In fact, the work of mapping out the library is concurrent with the work of renovating the library. One might say, a thing must be already gone in order to be mapped. One might say, this is also a metaphor. Or a convenience. Or a civilization.

There are seven new wings currently under construction, both above and below ground.

The Library is temperature-controlled. The exhibits cannot come into contact with sunlight, wind, air, human skin, or time.

There are four categories of exhibit in the library.

*

Categories in the Library

1. Named people with some reasonable explanation. These are people who, though missing, went missing under circumstances in which there is a plausible scenario for their disappearance and possible later sightings.

2. Named people with no explanation. These are people whose vanishing has remained inexplicable, referred to colloquially by staff as "thin airs."

3. Unnamed people. These people exist only in photographs, oral accounts, and objects, but the details of who they are remain murky enough that the Library cannot confidently assign an identity.

4. People discernable only through artifacts. This last category covers anyone who we know of only through physical traces such as hair, gloves, toys, watches, etc. What they left behind allows us to discern that they are missing.

*

Item #3479, Category 2, 1994

Briefcase

This was the last known possession of Horace Lysander, aged 46, who boarded a flight for Frankfurt on April 23rd, 1994. While the plane arrived safely, Lysander vanished somewhere over the Atlantic Ocean. Extensive searches of the aircraft revealed nothing. The case gave rise to a number of conspiracy theories persisting to this day. His disappearance is opaque, durable, comfortable, impossible.

This briefcase was his only luggage. It is empty.

His son is the noted anthropologist Bernard Lysander.

*

Item 368444, Category 4, 1877

Map

This map is unfinished.

There are no people on the map. Maps are adept at inferring that the people who inhabit a land matter less than the map itself, and so the map aids in the project of disappearance.

It is not known how this map is connected to the disappearance of a specific person, but as the map must have had an owner, we may assume a missing person (or missing people) that the map does not indicate.

There are tooth marks in the map, which may have come from an animal, or, possibly, indicate the cartographer's foolish wish to eat the world. The attempt was unsuccessful.

*

Item 64911, category 4, date unknown

Voice Box

Voice box. Colloquialism for larynx, the space in the throat in which sound is produced. One of the taken-for-granted parts of the body, unlike the heart, lungs, or spinal column. It is susceptible to damage from even a light blow.

Voice box. Colloquialism for a mechanical device inserted surgically into the throat of someone who has lost their own voice. This device enables them to speak, though the quality of speech is diminished.

Voice box. Colloquialism for anything capable of recording the human voice and replaying it at a later date.

Because this object is somewhat mangled, it is not possible to discern which of the above definitions adheres to it.

*

Item #47563, Category 1, 2003

Mirror

This hung in the hallway of Australian art forger Joshua Carr, who glanced at himself every day before leaving his home, idly summing himself up as though he were a stranger, his hand already reaching past his image that rose up before him, and grasping with clever fingers at the handle, swinging out into the future, assured. His wife watched him watch his own face; it was the last thing she saw him see. He left his house at 6:23 p.m. on October 5th, 2003, calling out as he shut the door that he would return by 9:30.

While a body has never been recovered, he is believed to have been the victim of the artist Stefan Vitric, who was enraged at the devaluation of his work brought about by Carr flooding the market with fakes.

This explanation was never proved, as Vitric himself vanished the same night.

*

Item #47564, Category 2, 2003

Wedding Ring

This was the property of celebrated Australian artist Stefan Vitric (see Item #47563). This ring was found, along with Vitric's clothes, on the beach near his house, suggesting that he had drowned himself. Vitric's husband, Donald Frame, has repeatedly insisted that this is impossible, citing Vitric's contempt for suicide as an aesthetic cliché, as well as the happiness of their life together. Vitric's effects were donated on the condition that they be classified as Category 2.

The scratch marks on the ring may indicate use of force, or that Vitric refused to remove it when doing the dishes.

*

Associative Disappearance

Some disappearances are not metaphors.

For a disappearance to have meaning, it must be remembered.

Some things, some bodies, are better remembered than others.

Sometimes, there is a question of violence. Sometimes violence is not in question.

Time can be construed as a kind of violence upon the body; it is not certain whether that is a metaphor. The same could be said of history.

Some disappearances are more common than others.

Some are anomalies, such as the disappearance of men like Ezekiel Mason.

These anomalous disappearances are seen as representative of disappearance, hence their status as metaphors.

This could be seen as itself a form of disappearance.

*

Item 89433, Category 4, date unknown

Compact

A circular plastic compact, painted gold, such as might be given as a present, perhaps to a young woman.

The mirror that was inset in the compact has been removed.

The experience of looking for the mirror that is not there is unsettling, as though an eye had been removed from a face.

This is related to the experience of feeling eyes on your back when in fact you are alone in a room, being convinced that there is someone walking beside you when no one is there, or hearing messages from your most beloved dead.

Also to phantom limb pain, in which, after the loss of the hand or foot, the injured person will experience pain in the limb that is no longer there, or attempt to perform gestures with the lost hand.

Also hearing knocks on the door or window, but when you look, nothing is there.

Also the possibility that consciousness may persist after death.

Also the desire to create archives in which everything and everyone that was ever missing may be collected and remembered.

Also the failure of that intention.

*

Item 773366, Category 3, 1974

Music Box

She collected things like this: things that played music, or looked like they should play music, cheap perfume samples in bottles shaped like hearts or doves or female hands.

Placed on the wooden floor of her room, it played loud enough to be heard from the other side of the shut door.

The music box was covered in cardboard, but she ripped it off. Underneath, it was exposed metal, bumps, and spiny edges.

Her mother played "White Christmas" for a month solid (even in the middle of the night), but not on the music box itself, because she said it gave her the creeps.

When Irving Berlin had the idea for "White Christmas" he yelled to his secretary: *I've just thought of the best song I've ever written! The best song anyone has ever written!*

Bing Crosby made his eldest son step on the scale every morning. If the boy was heavier than his father thought he should be, they went into the study. When there, the boy was made to drop his pants and was beaten with a studded belt that was kept for this purpose. The beating continued until the skin was broken and the first drop of blood appeared, and then his father stopped.

*

Item 732960, Category 4, date unknown

Marbles

When she was a child, she played by herself in the dirt backyard,
and the sky pinched white at the edges and the clouds modified
themselves above her according to their custom and she thought
herself, if she thought at all, entirely alone on the earth, even though
she could hear noises in the house behind her, and the marbles were
green glass like rows of eyes looking up from the dusty flat land, and
they had swirled centres like egg white dropped into a cup of hot
water, and she remembered those round weights as the weight of
her childhood (that cold clicking weight in her hand).

*

Item 9042422, Category 3, date unknown

Comb and Five Hairs

The woman who combed her hair with this comb was unhappy.

She lived alone.

She often argued with her mother, her two sisters, and her brother, even though she rarely saw them.

At night, she would pause on the stairs (the third or possibly fourth stair) after she turned the lights off on her way to bed and feel the silence that dwelt around her and inside her and even though most people would find this sad, she found this to be the most peaceful time of her day, when she was, as much as she could be, blessed.

*

On the Nature of Disappearance

When alone, I imagined myself as a person made of glass, so all my blood, pumping, could be seen.

At what point after a person vanishes does their absence become inevitable? So that, in considering the moment when they disappeared, it becomes impossible to imagine anything other than their disappearance.

Conversely, does this ever happen? Or is a moment of disappearance in fact a split in time, in which two things happen at once.

One thing: I have disappeared into nothing.

Or, I have entered into everything. The rustle of rats in the wall. The drip of a tap. A bad taste in the mouth, an abrupt alarming smell.

Walking alone, you come upon a single glove, or shoe, pressed into the light snow.

Or find a handprint on the wrong side of a windowpane.

Or find a collection of marbles, still grouped carefully together in the backyard.

Messages.

Providence

In which I talk with the doctor who cut open the chest of Jason Zirganos,
whose heart stopped during a marathon swim in the Irish Sea, 1958.

What he attempted was not necessary. We
are not necessary to the earth. The sea
didn't require him. His hypothermic flesh,
a pale stub shallow on the surface. The water
stayed grey, moving as interlocking plates
of metal. His body a chink in armour
that the arrow finds.

When did he die?

When we pulled him out, he was nearly dead, or was already
(I have kept quiet about this; who knows, even me, how to see
the last breath, knowing it is the last), but I had to try

because I had watched him from the boat for sixteen hours.
When he was just a guess in the dark, when he spat blood,
when he shot forward with the force of a blow to the head, his skin
contracted over him, the salt
burning all the soft tissue.

We got him up on the deck. He poured
fluid from his nose and mouth.

I loved him. I was at a loss.

He would seem nothing to these modern swimmers: unphotogenic,
unaided by science, flagging with late middle age, stamina
the closest he came to beauty. Outline

staining the space around him. The splutter
that might have been a death rattle, or phlegm spuming
from somewhere inside, his lungs
unshrivelling in the air.

What did his heart feel like?

Like any heart, like yours, stopped in your chest,
or mine, which is also stopped
now, as you must have guessed—

I'm dead, the event unmarked in *The New York Times*,
or even the Greek papers. The man who opened in vain
the chest of Jason Zirganos, it's not enough to merit
my own obituary.

I sliced him
with a penknife (my bloody,
bloody hands), we pumped
toward the shore, the rain
shrouding cliffs.

I addressed myself
to the future. Nothing answered.

What about the sea?

It was rage and indifference, before and after.
It swung him through open water,
past shoals, reefs, narrows, markers, anything that could
help him to distinguish his body from what was outside it.

He had nothing to go on, and he went.

Underwater, there is nothing we can know, nothing.

I wish I had left his heart alone. For years after
I woke with it smearing my hands. I weighed it.
Heavy as my wife's head, or our child, sleeping.

If I'd just thrown him back overboard. Only a body, heavy
as a sack of wet flour, let him turn over and over
in the wake of the boat.

The water would have swelled him like a sponge, his limbs
purple-and-green fronds, his hair
colonized by fish. Sediment settling through his pores,
his feet woven with seaweed. I would envy him.

Reading *The Oxford Book of Prayer*

(for my friend Dan, who has died)

Prayer

We were given
your books. A loan
from your husked-off years.

Wrote your name
on every flyleaf, hundreds
of times. When I sit
beside the shelves, there
you are. Speech
almost possible.

Oh Lord hear me,
I am in need.

I guess that's the substance
of prayer. If I were a praying person, not
a wishing one.

You owned this. Leafed
through it, attention snagged
here or there, but where
exactly, closed now.

I'm surprised by it. And not.
That this slipped into your hand.

Evidence
of faith: something hard,
inarguable, a stone in the shoe
four miles along an unpaved road.

Your possible faith is not
comforting. Enough
of comfort, anyway.

Christ with me

And what if you read

Christ before me

this in your room,

Christ behind me

stopping to look up
at the cracks in the paint
(monk-like hunch to your walk,
three inches of whiskey knocked back)

Christ in me

and keeping the window closed

Christ beneath me

against the noisy street, horns
and blown grit, gritted teeth

Christ above me

and you throw the book
without looking, sheets
piled beside you, greying on the unmade bed

Christ on my right
Christ on my left

and the book half-forgotten—an unfinished drink,
cigarette left burning—as you try to sleep.

Christ where I lie

Here, I am reading prayers—

Christ where I sit

in my late-night house, hoping
for proof
of you

Christ where I arise

like you were a conversation
still going on somewhere, my ear
cocked for your intimation: other
houses, other rooms.

If prayer is a way to see ghosts, I'll pray

Christ in the heart of every one who thinks of me
Christ in the mouth of every one who speaks of me
Christ in every eye that sees me
Christ in every ear that hears me

The man on the cover is not
kneeling—crouched heavily, someone
hunkering for a race.

Out of focus beside a river or ocean, palms
pressing knees, head bowed, so tired,
so lonely, he could be

anyone, any
one, you.

*

Pompeii

I dream you are the inhabitant of a distant town.
And I am a visitor, walking.
On the horizon, boiling sky, belch of liquid rock,
carnage. The bad spirits
coming home. I walk toward

while wishing to walk away. I am
immune to the heat, but
I have a body. You don't.
I look for you in each house.

By the time I get to you
the fires are out. All of them.
I step over a dog's bones

and find your image in a doorway—
outlined in ash, crouched.

A strong wind will scatter you.

*

Questions for the Dead

Did you know?

Did you know you knew?

Were you alone, or greeted, or alone, and then greeted
at the moment when you were most alone?

Was it light or dark?

Did you, for a second, become everything even
as, or just before, you became nothing?

Did you become nothing?

What kind of light was it?

What kind of darkness?

Did light and dark have a taste and texture, like food?

Did the sky open or close?

What was the first thing that happened,
after you were no longer afraid?

Notes and Acknowledgments

"I should have been a pair of ragged claws" is from T. S. Eliot's "The Love Song of J. Alfred Prufrock."

"'Housewife' Revised" is a reading of Anne Sexton's "Housewife."

Ann Lee was the founder of the Shakers, a group that espoused chastity, direct communication with God, and the equality of men and women. She claimed to have been, in her youth, examined by four ministers, speaking to them for four hours in seventy-two tongues.

Arnold Potter was the leader of a schismatic group of Latter Day Saints. In 1872, he led his followers to the edge of a cliff, announcing it was time for him to ascend to heaven, and leapt to his death.

William W. Davies was also the leader of a splinter group of Latter Day Saints. He founded a community called the Kingdom of Heaven in Washington, and claimed the divinity of himself and his two sons; the group dispersed after his sons died of diphtheria.

Laszlo Toth attempted to destroy Michelangelo's *Pietà* by attacking it with a geologist's hammer in 1972; he was declared insane and hospitalized for two years in Italy.

According to Roman legend, the Cumaean Sibyl offered nine books of prophecy to Tarquin the Proud, the last king of Rome. When he refused to meet her price, she burned three of the books, and offered him the remaining six for the same price. He still refused. She burned another three books. Desperate not to lose the prophecies entirely, Tarquin finally agreed to buy the last three books for the same price as the original nine.

All but the first of the quotations in "Reading *The Oxford Book of Prayer*" are from the prayer of St. Patrick.

*

Early versions of some of these poems appeared in *CV2, The Fiddlehead, Grain, The Literary Review of Canada, The Malahat Review,* and *Prairie Fire.* Thanks to the editors.

Thanks to everyone at Brick Books, particularly Barry Dempster, Marijke Friesen, Kitty Lewis, Alayna Munce, and my splendid, precise, and patient editor Helen Guri. You people pull it off with generosity, elegance, and grace, and somehow make it look easy.

Work on this book was supported at points by the Canada Council for the Arts and the Ontario Arts Council.

Thanks to Jessica Moore and Kilby Smith-McGregor, who critiqued much of what became the manuscript.

Thanks to the members of Zuppa Theatre, for their presence in the Pied Piper poems and, especially, "The Library of the Missing," which is connected to a collaborative work created with the company, *The Archive of Missing Things.*

Thanks to Dan DeMatteis, Senior, and Carol DeMatteis.

Thanks to Lea Ambros and to our kids.

Kate Cayley is the author of a previous poetry collection (*When This World Comes to an End*, Brick Books), a young adult novel (*The Hangman in the Mirror*, Annick Press), and a short story collection (*How You Were Born*, Pedlar Press), which won the 2015 Trillium Book Award and was a finalist for the Governor General's Award. She is a playwright-in-residence with Tarragon Theatre and has written two plays for Tarragon, *After Akhmatova* and *The Bakelite Masterpiece*. She lives in Toronto with her partner and their three children.